Thus Spoke Zerubbabel

Musings of a Mountain Preacher
A Smoky Mountain Version Based and Adapted from the
Book of Ecclesiastes

**"Sometimes life ain't much punkin'
but me and God will make do!"**

By Bruce W. Spangler

Dedication

To all my kin, both known and unknown.
To all those life teachers of the great Mystery,
many thanks!

Thus Spoke Zebediah

Musings of a Mountain Preacher
A Smoky Mountain Version Based and Adapted from the
Book of Ecclesiastes

"The unexamined life is not worth living."
Socrates

"But the examined life makes you wish you were dead."
William P. Brown
Ecclesiastes Interpretation: A Bible Commentary for Teaching and Preaching

"Did you ever say Yes to a single joy? Oh, my friends, then you said Yes to all woe as well. All things are chained together, entwined, in love."
Friedrich Nietzsche
Thus Spoke Zarathustra

"Sometimes life ain't much punkin' but me and God will make do!"
Musings of a Mountain Preacher

A Wound and a Port of Call

Life in Appalachia carries its stereotypes.

As it is known among us from Appalachia, in particular the southern region, we work really hard to earn every last one. We are probably the most religious folks on earth with a natural bent towards cursing a blue streak all the while "praising God."   We are "god-fearing" and "feared" by the outsider, especially if the encounter with one of us is accompanied by the faint yet distinct sound of banjo music, or so goes one of the many stereotypes.

Tom Wingo, of Pat Conroy's **Prince of Tides,** declares that his "wound is geography and his anchorage, his port of call."

My ancestors hail and descent from those Europeans who made their way west to this land of Uncle Sam searching for God knows what but sure to make their claim when they found it.   They ended up in southern Appalachia in a region now known as the Smoky Mountains.

The land, the ridges, the mountains and the life therein claimed them and continue to do so with all their subsequent offspring. Southern Appalachia became both their wound and anchorage, as well as mine.

I am rich with the heritage passed down through generations by a few known characters and plenty of unknowns. The rich legacy left behind is the currency of stories filled with tales of courage and cowardly acts, inspiration and despair, love and hate. Stories that stretch the truth but will never stray far from it. Stories of individuals who were strong and tall as Georgia pines yet would shed a tear at the drop of hat. Stories that are painted with characters and individuals - men and women - who have made the ancient yet always contemporaneous existential journey from youthful undisciplined zeal towards a maturation of a life lived amidst the landscape of the mystery of faith, while tucked away in the ridges and hollers of these southern mountains.

All peoples, all cultures have their way of conveying this pilgrimage, of this life's journey towards authentic living. All cultures offer the invitation to take the first step. This journey towards claiming one's life and living in its fullest always begins with a litany of questions.

What does it mean to be human?

What is the essence of life in light of certain death?

Is there a payoff for a "good life?"

Is there a day of reckoning in living a life where I "ain't so good?"

When and where does the skin of innocence shed?

In what or whom can I find a sense of safety, security and/or certainty?

Is such a pursuit worthy?

Necessary?

Possible?

Wise?

Should I even care?

What if I want to be a hero?

Famous?

Both?

What would I gain?

What do I lose?

The stories passed down encompass such questions, offering a variety of answers yet always provoking more questions.

From the wisdom literature of the Hebrew Bible comes Qoheleth, the preacher or teacher of the book of Ecclesiastes who, as well, provides some musings about life and such questions.

Scholarship suggests that Ecclesiastes contains the musings of a sage, a teacher of wisdom but collected, recorded and now preserved by one of the Teacher's students. Attempting to capture the "musings" of the wise elder, the student scribbles his/her notes for later study, contemplation, and examination. Wisdom, however, possesses no magic or special powers. Knowledge is only the leftover musings of a life lived; yet wisdom is what experience leaves behind both in a life endured and life held in awe. Life is more than just what I know. It is how I live with what I may or may not know. Living life, while informed of the sure and certain knowledge of death, does incline one to measure all the "footsteps" of existence. Confronting one's mortality does put some things into perspective.

Life does end.

We do die.

We do not have a choice about whether we die. We, however, do have the choice to live and enter into the mystery of life, suggests Qoheleth. In so doing, we may catch a glimpse of the Divine along the way. We may even conclude or sense that the Divine has always had an eye on us.

As some Appalachians will attest, life can be quite hilarious as expressed often through self-debasing humor that is so common and prevalent among us. We all hope, that in catching a glimpse of the Divine during our lifetime, that God would do the same to us as God did to Moses – expose the Divine "backside!" Full moons need not always be lunar! Sometimes the response to life exceeds a verbal response. Such a Divine "mooning" is not so such a gesture of indifference or sophomoric revelry but a metaphysical backhanded wave of an invitation to "follow me into the full mystery of life."

Socrates, the Greek philosopher, invites humanity on the journey to move from the landscape of naiveté to a much richer land of self-awareness. Life is far from engaging and intriguing if one fails to discover the authentic self.

Ecclesiastes invites us to leave the land of naiveté and innocence as well. However, the examined life has a home where it abides. That land or country is known as mystery. You can never claim mystery; it can only claim you. Now I understand why my ancestors found these mountains both a wounding and an anchorage.

What if Qoheleth is suggesting that authentic living is a life journey with mapped points beginning with innocence and emotional naiveté and then moving or drifting towards entering and engaging the mystery of life as a deliberate and intentional choice?

Continuing this journey of maturation, Qoheleth leads us through the forests and thickets of magic and naiveté in order to bring us to higher ground - to the land of mystery where freedom and life are experienced through the daily grind of life yet articulated through the language vehicle of faith. Cursing a blue streak may just be the most sincere form of prayer since Job insisted that surely God must be held accountable as us humans. Maybe Moses' glimpse of God's backside was God's response to Job's demand. Faith may consider any Divine mooning akin to a splash of cold and frigid mountain water to garner our attention and awake us from both the slumber and stupor of a life half lived.

So in true southern Appalachian form, I offer a Smoky Mountain Version of the book of Ecclesiastes. I offer at best a paraphrase and at worst, an embellishment of this ancient book through my own musings about life. I'll be that transparent.

Some may find my musings nothing more than tasteless and hard as brickbat peaches. Yet, even in Appalachia, we find a use for such peaches. We call them pie-peaches. You never throw anything away; you recycle. Just as Ecclesiastes may have recycled the journey of Enkidu in the Epic of Gilgamesh[1], I do the same with Qoheleth. In the Sumerian epic of Gilgamesh, the mythical "wild man" Enkidu is "nurtured" from a wild brute of a primitive to a man who matures to adulthood, claiming his rightful place in civilized society. Yet we all replay this ancient epic when we examine our lives and explore what it means to be human. What it means to claim or reject our roles in community. We recycle our lives at the moment we acknowledge our own breath in this cold and fading mist we call a lifetime. Vanity. Vanity. All is vanity. Even Qoheleth suggests that life is so short lived, so short that to close one's eyes in before the mist of life; one just may miss it all.

My life is defined by the geography of the Smoky Mountains. It is where I begin and it keeps calling me towards this mysterious place, claiming my life and proposing that I do the same.

Ecclesiastes begins with a bold declaration.

"Vanity of vanities...vanity of vanities! All is vanity."

This declaration may parallel Friedrich Nietzsche's "greatest weight."

In his book, **The Gay Science**, Nietzsche provides a thought experiment.

---

[1] William P. Brown, Ecclesiastes. *Interpretation: A Bible Commentary for Teaching and Preaching*. (Louisville: John Knox Press, 2000), see 2-7.

"What, if some day or night a demon were to steal after you into your loneliest loneliness and say to you: 'This life as you now live it and have lived it, you will have to live once more and innumerable times more; and there will be nothing new in it, but every pain and every joy and every thought and sigh and everything unutterably small or great in your life will have to return to you, all in the same succession and sequence—even this spider and this moonlight between the trees, and even this moment and I myself. The eternal hourglass of existence is turned upside down again and again, and you with it, speck of dust!'

Would you not throw yourself down and gnash your teeth and curse the demon who spoke thus? Or have you once experienced a tremendous moment when you would have answered him: 'You are a god and never have I heard anything more divine.' If this thought gained possession of you, it would change you as you are or perhaps crush you. The question in each and every thing, 'Do you desire this once more and innumerable times more?' would lie upon your actions as the greatest weight. Or how well disposed would you have to become to yourself and to life to crave nothing more fervently than this ultimate eternal confirmation and seal?" Aphorism 341.

Nietzsche makes plenty of declarations throughout all his writings. However, this weightier matter of recurrence and accepting and embracing a repeated life of joy and woe is more than just pondering. It is worth confronting.

Is the book of Ecclesiastes making a similar claim on life? Is the book a blunt assertion that every act of life, every detail of it - every viewed sunset and observed moonlight - is just a repeat of a repeat of a repeat?

Is the epilogue (12:13-14) of Ecclesiastes a bold yet orthodox theological declaration attempting to retort the Nietzsche's demon? Or is Qoheleth actually embracing the god of such recurrence?

Nietzsche is known for his bold and heretical but yet prophetic declaration that "God is dead." Yet, he may be suggesting that the examined life warrants a perspective that sees the world as a "dance-floor for Godlike accidents...Gods' table for Godlike dice and dice-throwers."[2]

---

[2] Thus Spoke Zarathustra, 3.4.

Without the epilogue of Ecclesiastes, one might make the argument that Qoheleth reaches the same conclusion that humanity no longer has need of the Divine, and thus echoes that "God is dead."   If the epilogue is the editorial work of a young student, does it represent the limited if not somewhat immature posturing of one yet to experience the pains and joys, grief and pleasures of a full life?   Every student, in the beginning, wants to insure that the Teacher does not stray too far from the fold of a magical world.

What if everything is repeated?

How do I respond?

Even my birth is a response.

Even my birthplace is a response.

If I do not examine my life, that, too, is a response.

My response, in addition, has a context. A place where I begin, explore and live and die.   Place is just as important in examining life.

As a side product of being Appalachian, I am quite versed on limiting my opportunities on life, thus my wound.

Yet, there can be no vanities until there is human life. There can be no life until there is place to live out life.   The book of Genesis makes this point. Place is important. Place is context. It is where I stand. Everyone must stand some place. So I begin **Thus Spoke Zebediah** with a Smoky Mountain Version of Creation as a declaration that in the end I must conclude that sometimes life ain't much punkin' but me and God will make do.

If the world for Nietzsche is a dance floor or table for throwing dice, then the world of Appalachia is place of "buck dancing" and "farming."   My ancestors seem to know of no other types of dancing or gambling. To introduce the playground of this Smoky Mountain Version of Ecclesiastes, imagine the story of creation (Genesis 1) as "Chickens Roosting and Roosters Crowing."

"Chickens Roosting and Roosters Crowing"
A Smoky Mountain Version of Genesis Chapter One

As only God could, God commenced to create a place for the clouds above and a place below for the soil of the fields.

And the fields were without seed - never touched by hand or plow; and a dusky and dark desolation hovered over the raging rivers, but God's passion for life came over the waters.

Then God said, "Let there be brightness." And there was brightness.

And God saw that the brightness was downright good. It was so good; it was like enjoying a glass of iced-tea under the shadow of a tall oak on a hot August afternoon.

So God made a difference between the brightness and the dusk; God hooped and hollered because of the brightness of day; to the dusk, God praised it as night. This first day was one of chickens roosting and roosters crowing.

Then God said, "Let there be an upside-down wash tub betwixt the waters above and the waters below that they be different."

So God formed a big washtub, a real big one, mind ya. God turned it upside down and separated the waters under the tub from the waters above the tub.

No fooling!

No kidding!

God called that upside down washtub the sky above. And just like the first day, the second day was of one of chickens roosting and roosters crowing.

God went on to say, "Let the waters under the sky be 'shooed' to one place and let the once flooded land appear."

No fooling!

God call the once flooded land – the fields; and God called the gathered waters – the Mississippi.

That was good, indeed.

And God thought about having a mess of homemade apple cobbler with that glass of iced-tea.

God said again (for God loves to talk), "Let the fields sprout all sorts of greenery. But no kudzu! Let there be plants with seeds, fruit trees of all kinds because we just might want a cobbler or two."

No fooling!

The fields brought forth all things green. Still there was no kudzu; it comes later, much later because it doesn't need much time to run! The land birthed and nourished trees bearing apples, cherries, peaches, and the like, all with seeds in them.

So God baked an apple cobbler because God was tickled pink with everything.

And just like the previous ones, this third day was one of chickens roosting and roosters crowing.

God went and said, "Let there be lights in the upside down tub of the sky to know the difference between day and night; and let them be signs for planting, harvesting and dressing hogs. They will be signs for golden leaves, snow covered fields, sowing seed and tall corn. These lights will shine on the fields like a momma's smile and gaze upon her newborn."

No fooling!

And God made them lights.

The big one was for the day, and the smaller one was to take care of the night and the stars.

So God stuck them in the upside down washtub of the sky to shine as God seen fit and to care for the day and the night, making a difference between daylight and dusk.

All this was so pleasing to God.

The smell of apple cobbler baking filled the hollers and ridges as a bouquet of spring flowers.

And yep, just like the other days, this day was one of chickens roosting and roosters crowing.

So God said, "Let the waters birth plenty of small lively water animals and creatures." God never dreamed that the little snail darter would be the most famous. God also said, "Let the birds soar above the land and fields, flying across the upside down washtub of the sky."

So God did.

And God created the bigger water animals and all living creatures that creep, of every kind, that fill the waters and all the winged birds of every kind.

So God scooped a mess of that apple cobbler.

It's hard to believe that life could get any better.

Moved by it all, God stooped down to the footstool of God's living room called the Smoky Mountains and blessed all them animals, fish, and especially the snail darter, saying, "Be abundant, be many, and fill these waters and creeks and streams and rivers. Let the birds be many in the fields and the skies."

And this fifth day was really one of chickens roosting and roosters crowing.

Then God said, "Let the fields feed the living things of every kind, the cattle and horses, the goats and sheep, chickens and roosters, and even the bugs, and all that walks and crawls on the earth, each of every kind. And dog-gone-it, this was so pleasing that God looked around for someone to share cobbler and iced-tea.

"I don't want to always eat and drink by my lonesome. I'm going to invite kin. Yep, let's invite kinfolk to be in these hills and fields and they shall be my people," God said.

(God and God's kin look alike, you know.)

And God went on to say more, "My people will enjoy and care for the fish of the waters, the birds of the sky, and the cattle and horses, goats and sheep, chickens and roosters, bugs of all kinds."

So God made preparations for family.

God's family will be people of the land, fields and mountains, who resemble God. And just like God, they were prepared – all were prepared the same, the women and men, all equal.

Again, God stooped at the footstool, welcoming and blessing the people, saying, "Be abundant, be many and fill the fields, take good care of it. Enjoy and nurture the fields, the birds, and the cattle and horses, the goats and sheep, and even the bugs.

Furthermore, God said to them, "Lookie! I have given you all the plants that produce seed in its fruit that is upon the flats and hills of this land. From the trees you shall have shelter, buckets, canoes and a fiddle or two."

No fooling!

So God saw all that had been made and prepared. It was really good. And yes, it is nice to share cobbler and tea with kinfolk.

This was the sixth day of chickens roosting and roosters crowing.

And now the heavens, the fields, hills, streams, creeks, rivers and mountains, all of God's creation were complete, everything!

With creation finished and just beginning, God rocked and relaxed on the big screened-in-porch on that day of rest. Rocking, God began to wonder about things to come, trying to envision the fields, hills, and mountains come mid-June and early July.

God is a dreamer, you know.

Finished from creating the world, or otherwise known as Appalachia, God said that this seventh day was special because everything was good.

And so God rested, rocking, on the front porch.

This is the story of beginnings.

Yep, this is the story of the creation of the Smoky Mountains.

This Smoky Mountain Version of Ecclesiastes if about finding myself on that front porch! That porch is my port of call!

Thus Spoke Zebediah
Musings of a Mountain Preacher
A Smoky Mountain Version Based and Adapted from the
of the Book of Ecclesiastes

Prologue

The year was 2001 and Zebediah (God's gift) had been living on Rich Mountain in the Smoky Mountains near Townsend, Tennessee. After ten years of solitary study and meditation in a tucked away mountain cave, Zebediah felt called by the great Mystery to come down from the mountain to share what was on this mind and heart. He realized from the outset that folks would be fixed on their own ways and their own ways of thinking and doing things. He wasn't descending from the mountain to gather up a following.

No, he was coming down because he was a little tired of listening to himself all these years and began wondering if others might have some of the same ponderings about life and death and death and life as he. His conclusion about life is rather simple: "Sometimes life ain't much punkin' but me and God will make do!"

Zebediah often felt as though God done forgot God's part and that everything had been put into his own hands. This came to him in a dream one night.

He dreamed that a book salesman came one day to the mountain cave where he had made his home for several years. The salesman opened a book to read to ignite a sale, "What if some day or night a demon were to steal after you into your loneliest loneliness and say to you: 'This life as you now live it and have lived it, you will have to live once more and innumerable times more' ... Would you not throw yourself down and gnash your teeth and curse the demon who spoke thus? Or have you once experienced a tremendous moment when you would have answered him: 'You are a god and never have I heard anything more divine.'"

The book salesman then added, "I only have one book to sell. Are you interested?"

Zebediah then awoke from his dream.

The next morning, Zebediah left that mountain and made his way to Knoxville.   There he became the preacher at Crooked Creek Congregation of the Tired but True Believers Church.   These are his weightier musings and ponderings on a life lived and examined.

1.1

I've been pondering...says the preacher from the Crooked Creek Congregation of the Tired but True Believers.

1.2

Life is like the morning mist covering Crooked Creek.   Yep, life disappears quicker than the morning mist.   Ain't much to it, so it seems.

1.3

What do we as humans got to show for our grubbing around? Working our fingers to the bone, working before daylight until the middle of the moon's light?

1.4

A bunch of young'ns come, a bunch of young'ns come of age, and bunch of young'ns get old, a bunch of young'ns die but Crooked Creek stays around like an iron anvil.

1.5

The rooster crows and the sun run to its place, dusk and dawn.

1.6

The breath of the Almighty Mystery blows indiscriminately wherever it wants; it comes and goes from all the four corners.

1.7

Crooked Creek runs to the river, but the river never gets full; Crooked Creek always runs but never runs out.

1.8

Life is the workinest and wearinest thing, no rest for those who are weary; the eye takes hold of something only to want to see something else; the ear takes in the world all the while waiting on the next sound.

1.9

I don't reckon that I ain't seen and done most everything under in this short life; some days I wish there was more – more things, more kinfolks, more life.

1.10

They say that the Sears and Roebuck catalog has something new each year, but I don't think so. It's just the same old stuff, just different color. Life is that way too. Same book, same pages, same people doing the same ole stuff.

1.11

We are quick to forget our upbringing and those doing the upbringing because we are looking for something new, something novel. We are always eager, too impatient. We settle for new wine in new skin. We settle for shine before the final run.

1.12

I, the Preacher, have been at Crooked Creek ever since my calling.

1.13

And I have been a'think'n ever since about what this life is supposed to mean. I been a'think'n' real hard and hardly think'n; either way I ain't got it figgered just yet. I know what I know and that seems to be about all God has trusted me with and probably you too.

1.14

I've been the workinest and weariest of mankind all my life and done seen it all. Life is like the morning mist covering Crooked Creek. Yep, life disappears quicker the morning mist. Ain't much to it, so it seems.

1.15

You can't make Crooked Creek straight. I don't care what TVA gots to say. And when you add nothing to nothing, you get double that!

1.16

I said to myself, "Momma didn't raise any fool. I know the difference between a loaf of bread and a Rhode Island Red. I've been round long enough to know the difference. I've learned a thing or too since my upbringing."

1.17

I'm nobody's fool. But no matter how much I know, it doesn't add one minute longer to the morning mist. It doesn't add one more minute to life. The preacher over my grave ain't going to say to the grave diggers, "Boys don't throw the dirt on him just yet; by his watch he has another minute coming!" No, it just ain't that way!

1.18

Sometimes I just wish I could be content as a spring flower, but I ain't. Thus spoke Zebediah.

2.1

But one day I said to myself, "If I ain't content, then I'd just as well grab hold of some fun while I'm waiting." Mind you, however, fun was fun but it didn't last. It was gone quicker than the morning mist over Crooked Creek.

2.2

Life will give you something to laugh about. Give it a moment or two, however, and before you know it, you are crying or hurting - or both.

2.3

I had heard that a dram of whiskey might cheer a poor body's soul, so the wisdom went.   Maybe whiskey can help get one through the waiting until the contentment comes one's way, so the wisdom went.

2.4

If whiskey doesn't help, maybe keeping my hands busy during the waiting would do it. Pappy always said, "Idle hands are the devil's workshop."

2.5

So I got busy. I planted some sweet potatoes and peach trees.

2.6

I drawed creek water to give drink to my sweet potatoes and peach trees.

2.7

Why stop there, I said to myself, so I raised some milk cows and a pig or two.   Everybody done started talking about how my sweet potatoes and peaches growed so quickly. "Sweetest milk and spiciest pork sausage this side of Wear's Valley," everyone used to say about what I got out of my cows and pigs.

2.8

Why law, I ended up with more money than Uncle Sam but something was missing from my life. Music! Music, yes that was what I was missing. So I bought me a fiddle and learned how to play mighty fine.

2.9

Before long, everybody thought that I was the next best thing to come along since sliced white bread.   People came from all the hollers to talk to me and give ear to my music. That's when I first sensed my calling to preaching.

2.10

The harder I worked and made music the more I got. When you get famous and rich everyone thinks you have the insights to life and they come to you for advice and counsel.

2.11

Then I got to thinking again about being content; I wasn't. In spite of all those sweet potato pies, sweet milk and spicy sausage biscuits, I still was awaiting for contentment. I had gained nothing. After all the work with the peaches, everybody said that they were only fit for pie-peaches because they were so hard and woody. All my work, just not the peaches, felt as though I had tried to grab hold of the morning mist over Crooked Creek.   I grabbed hold but it just slipped through my fingers.

2.12

So I got back to pondering about contentment.

2.13

I was told as a young'n that it's best to be thought a fool than to speak and remove all doubt.   So I keep most ponderings to myself.

2.14

Just because you got eyes in your head don't mean that you can walk in the dark.   Whether you got life smarts or school smarts, everyone is after the same – contentment.

2.15

So does it matter to be thought a fool or everybody knows it for sure? Either way, you still find yourself waiting for contentment. Fool or not, the morning mist over Crooked Creek is gone by afternoon.

2.16

A hundred years from now, when someone looks at my headstone, will they be able to tell whether I was a fool or not. Nobody will be around to rescue my name sake.

2.17

So is life worth living? Little Katie didn't think so when she got full growed. I thought about the same. Life is like the gray, gloomy shade of a morning mist over Crooked Creek.

2.18

With bony fingers I will go to my grave and the payday for all my hard work will be my young'ns buying all the fanciest new gadgets from the Sears and Roebuck catalogue. I don't know if that is any good or not.

2.19

Will they be fools or not? It is up to them, I reckon. Yet I'll be the one with bony fingers and they won't. Damn that mist!

2.20

I just gave into the idea that this is the way life is lived.

2.21

Sometimes the children's teeth are not set on edge but they get to eat prime rib at Regas. They get it with sweet tea every week because I was so smart. Crooked Creek!

2.22

So will all the things that hard work can wrought bring about contentment?

2.23

The hard work brings crooked fingers and crooked backs and restless minds;   Life is just a mist.

2.24

If you are going to work hard all your life, you better learn how to live life hard as well.   This must be the way God intended.

2.25

Reckon God just fixed it that way.

2.26

Sometimes life is really generous. Sometimes life takes away more than it gives. Some days life is fair. Other days, it ain't. Go catch the morning mist over Crooked Creek before you tell why life is fair and ain't fair.

Thus Zebediah spoke.

3.1

It is said that the fork in the road can take us one of two ways, and it usually does.

3.2

The start of all things and the end of all things; even death creates beauty, so echoes the professor from the University of Tennessee;

3.3

There is a time to quit life, and another time to make sure it continues; there is a time to tear down a fence line, there is a time to build one, too;

3.4

There are days that it is best to shed a tear out of grief, and a time to shed a tear out of sheer joy; there is wailing, and then there is time for fiddle and clogging;

3.5

There is a time to leave stones a'layin', and a time to pick them and pile them together; a time to hug, and a time to just shake hands.

3.6

A time to fetch and a time to send off; a time to keep what is in your pocket, and another time to empty your pocket;

3.7

There is time to use scissors, and another time to use the sewing needle.   Know when to incline your ear and when to be wordy;

3.8

A time to love, and a time to love in a different way; resist fighting and hold out for serenity.

3.9

In the big scheme of things, why are we here?

3.10

I've been around these mountains long enough to know the hand that has been dealt to us. But who is doing the dealing?

3.11

God's work among us is quite mysterious; though we can experience that mystery, we just can't get a hold of it. It gets hold of us but though we try, we can't return the grip.

3.12

If I was dealing the hand, I would want everyone to know that they are in the hands of a happy God!

3.13

There is something about working the land and eating the fruits of one's labor. I'd rather not have pie-peaches, but I'd still eat them if they are in a pie!

3.14

Whatever God is up to, it ends up feeling like love. I reckon that God wants everyone to feel loved. Yep, I know that is what God wants!

3.15

In the end, I guess the best thing to do is to respect the Mystery.

3.16

Just when I think justice will have its day, wickedness gets its say. Just when I think I know what wickedness looks like and I'm about to call it out, justice speaks and says, "No, it's me." Most of the time, I just can't tell the difference between the sprout and weeds.

3.17

I reckon that I have learned some patience and not be so quick to weed. Maybe God knows a little more than me about such things.

3.18

Maybe Aristotle was right, we, people, are just rational animals. Maybe God just wants us to realize such a notion.

3.19

In the end, whether we are rational or not, we die just like any critter. Though we may be able to think, humans and critters still just need to breathe.

In that regards, humans have no advantage.   It reminds me of the mist hovering over Crooked Creek.

3.20

To the ground we all go and return to the dust where we first began.

3.21

Does my dog Beau have a soul? Will we both get the chance to run the white mountain meadow rue of the life beyond?   Or is this all we get on this side of the Great Smoky Mountains?

3.22

Reckon if I plan on doing all my living on the other side of life, I will probably miss out on a lot of living here in these mountains.
Thus spoke Zebediah.

4.1

Speaking of this world, there are too many heartaches and pains for us humans for my comfort. Too many people left with too much heartache and not enough comfort. More tears than handkerchiefs. Furthermore, it looks like the Golden Rule gets the first and last word in my neck of the woods – those who turn the lumber and coal into gold get to make all the rules.

4.2

At least in the grave the Golden Rulers ain't got any say - unless my grave is in the way of lumber and coal!   Sometimes it feels as though I expect help from God against God.   For those Golden Rulers will be the first to say that they are "God-fearers" and helping folks out.

4.3

Some days I just think that the grave holds less heartache and more grace than the cradle.

The cradle holds a lot of promise with the innocence but becomes tainted in living life.

4.4

Why is it that my heart and mind wants the fanciest of things in Johnson Holler only because someone else has them? It ain't because of I am in dire need that I want it. I didn't know that I wanted it until I went to Johnson Holler. I am funny that way and so seems many others. Is my life just a bundle of wants that I observe others having? God, I hope not! If so, then life ain't anything but a wood chip or a piece of coal.

4.5

Am I just a shallow fool? Do I play the role without effort?   When will I be more than a wood chip or a lump of coal?

4.6

A fool just may be one who has taken the time to get to know oneself. Even the ole trickster Jacob got a new name when he was honest with himself by wrestling with the great Mystery.

4.7

And another thing that is like dust in a whirlwind...

4.8

Living as though you ain't got any kin! Living as though wood and coal is my momma or daddy, or my brother or sister, or my second cousin is more than dust in the wind. It makes one unhappy.

4.9

There ain't any life without kin. There ain't any life if I don't insist on sipping on tea and eating apple cobble with company.

4.10

I imagine myself on Abrams Falls tripping on root and breaking my leg. If I fall, who will help me home?

If I yell and there is no one to hear me, am I even making a sound?

4.11

Everyone knows that two dogs will get you through a cold winter's night better than a single kiver.

4.12

My daddy told me that you can't play catch by yourself. If you do, it is a wearisome task!

4.13

Money and fame can't cover up a foolish heart. Just as you can't buy homegrown tomatoes and love, you can't buy wisdom.

4.14

Poverty can't buy you wisdom, either. Just because you are poor don't make you a fool just as gold doesn't make you wise.

4.15

There ain't any difference in people. We might have a different port called home or an unlike heartache but they don't make no better or worse than the other.

4.16

That is the way it has always been, here in these mountains and back in the old country. When we forget that we share the same history and live out the same history, then all of us are in trouble!
We ain't got much more sense than the morning mist at Crooked Creek. We are leaning our ladders up against the wrong wall.
Though my kin can't live my life, I need not neglect the wisdom of kin. Old man Twain said it best, "When I was a boy of fourteen, my father was so ignorant I could hardly stand to have the old man around. But when I got to be twenty-one, I was astonished by how much he'd learned in seven years." Thus Zebediah spoke.

5.1

There ain't any magic in a house of God. Both the insiders and its critics forget that there is only Mystery. Respect the Mystery that is all you can do. You can't hold it or demand something of it.   Respect the Mystery.

5.2

Don't let your mouth overload what you can't deliver, in all cases.

5.3

A foolish dream is filled with many words, empty ones at that.   If you meet someone who will use a thousand words when ten will do, like most politicians and many preachers, excuse yourself – any excuse will do! And do it in a hurry before you are in a whirlwind of meaningless jabber.

5.4

So don't use a thousand words when ten will suffice, with your neighbor, kinfolk or even the Mystery. Many words offend most of us, including the Mystery.

5.5

If a five dollar bill is in your wallet, don't say that it's a ten spot.

5.6

Remember that virtue proclaimed is not virtue gained.

5.7

Dream on, Dreamer.   Dream for and in this life, not the next!

5.8

The heavy hand of hate and bigotry has slapped many a folk in my day. Though the hand is often gloved in velvet, it does not remove the sting. Surely something can be done about such hate.

5.9

The poor need a good king.   The rich demand no king.

5.10

The food that money buys surely satisfies the belly. Money for the sake of money, on the other hand, is a menace to both the mind and the belly.

5.11

Do we know when enough is enough? Have you heard of the little mountain boy who was so full of chocolate gravy that he tried to put the remaining in his belly button? Must we live in a world of scarcity?   All this chasing after the whirling dust of more makes my head swim.

5.12

Contentment comes from within not without. If I seek the gold for gold's sake, I will spent all my waking hours and some of my sleeping ones worrying who is plotting to take it away from me.

5.13

Remember this: you can't hold a baby with your arms full.

5.14

You only go away with an arm full of nothing.

5.15

We leave this life the same way we come – buck naked, bare butt to the world.

5.16

Imagine spending all your life chasing after the illusive mist of Crooked Creek.   All the planning and plotting will not keep the mist from seeping between the fingers of the grasping hand.   Then, what are we left with? Name it!

5.17

Anger?

Resentment?

Name it!

I dare you!

5.18

Imagine being chased by a mountain lion to an unforeseen cleft. As you peer over the cleft you see a black bear below. Between the charging lion and the bear below you feel trapped until out of the corner of your eye, the glistening blackness of a berry captures both your eye and appetite. There among the brush, you see the biggest blackberry ever! You reach for the berry and pop it into your mouth and declare, "Life can't get any better than this!"

5.19

This is the gift of God.

5.20

With the berries of life, time flies!
Thus spoke Zebediah.

6.1

Is it a mystery or is it a crime that the children's teeth are not set on edge by the parent's sour grapes?

6.2

But someone gets to eat the chocolate of life that is earned and paid for by another. Chocolate never sets one's teeth on edge but we want more! Is it better to die than to live? Should we die to live and live to die?

Are we willing to consider that everything in life gets repeated time and time again, same event, same sequence, same life, over and over again?

6.3

If the heavens boom with these words would we exclaim, "Get behind me Satan" or bow in adoration and declare, "Surely this is the living God!" What are the characteristics of a still born life? Which is better, a living death or a dying life?

6.4

Oh for the fear of the darkness of both the soul and heart. We would rather drink from the shallow spring of ignorance than reach into the deepest and darkest well that will quench my thirst for life!

6.5

Does the darkness bring rest to the weary?

6.6

We all die. We all give up the ghost! We all go out of this world buck naked but will we enjoy the ride?

6.7

All my labors are to feed my belly but I get hungry again within hours. What for am I really hungry?

6.8

Who is to say that the wise are not foolish?

Who is not to say that the fool is full of wisdom?

Are folly and wisdom just the different sides of the same coin? Is the fool and wise just the different sides of own myself?

6.9

The Doctor of the King set his eyes on the prize not for just the sake of himself and his family, but for all of us.

I don't care what the velvet gloves do!

6.10

All things will be repeated. Each of us will repeat our lives, every detail, and every sequence. Nothing then is really new! What then? Can we dispute the Mystery?

6.11

Sure, we have given all our words to dispute the Mystery, we name the Mystery to remove the cloak but where has it gotten us?   Do we finally declare, "All is straw!"

6.12

What is life?
A shadow?
A mind game?
A throw of the dice?
A dance?
Who will reveal it all?
When we give up the ghost will it then be revealed?
When my life is repeated, surely that is when I will know?
Surely, someone knows!
I'll go back to Crooked Creek in the morning to grasp the mist!
Thus Zebediah spoke.

7.1

A self made is better than all the gold of the world. A good name goes along with good shine. Is it really true that the deathbed holds less heartache than the birthing bed?

7.2

McCarthy's Funeral Home always meant a new haircut for my grandfather. Did he get a hair cut at the announcement of the birth of a grandbaby? We all do die but how many deaths? Death can only be heavy for the living.

7.3

The brokenness of life is the avenue to life anew. It can teach us much about living and it can make a heart glad in a sort of a paradoxical way. When I am at the end of rope, I see what is really important to and for me.

7.4

Don't run from your brokenness. Run right into it. Don't deny the power of your tears. Only the fool never cries. The bigger fool cries but never tastes of their healing salve.

7.5

Learn the songs of life from those who have lived it not from the fool who sings of observing life.

7.6

If you think that the flame from the kindling will keep burning and keep you warm, you are fooling yourself. If you think that the morning mist of Crooked Creek will cover today's problems, think again. Don't be vain!

7.7

Tell the truth but always with love.

7.8

Life is like a ride to Gatlinburg. Some enjoy the scenery along the way. Others only can't wait to get there. Many can't wait to get out of there. Patience will never get us from one place to another but at least it is good company.

7.9

Live by the adage: Do no harm!   Do good! Respect the Mystery!

7.10

Yesterday is always without sorrow. It is always perfect in the eyes of those who look back. It doesn't mean that tomorrow is better than today. Besides, you can live yesterday because it is always a day and tomorrow never comes.

7.11

Wisdom can come as a hand me down. A wise student only comes from a wise teacher.

7.12

Protect your wisdom and treat it like pearls; never cast it before swine. You can put pearls on a pig but it is still a pig; and besides, the pearls will only aggravate it.

7.13

Respect the Mystery. Respect its power. Respect its coming and going. Sometimes it comes right at you and other times it sneaks up and gooses you.

7.14

In the day of happiness, revel in its tears of joy. In the days of woe, revel in its tears of sorrow. They are all chained together, strung together like pearls, chained and strung with love.

7.15

In the shallowness of heart I have seen good people die young doing good and evil people live long doing their evil thing. Then again, I have seen good people live long doing good and evil people die quickly because of their evil doing. I want to make something of it but it seems that good people and evil people are often one in the same boat. Go figure.

7.16

No need to be a pompous intellectual or a pompous ass. It is even worse to be all three. Eventually, the pompous gets kick from under us and there is not much left either way.

7.17

Dead heroes never get to take their next breathe and are soon forgotten. A fool is ignored but seldom forgotten. No need to experience a public death until its time.

7.18

Momma said that you should use both hands with riding your bicycle. Letting go of the handle bars might make you wreck, she would say. What does she know? I've never seen her on a bike. But I do know that when she hugs me it is with both arms and hands.

7.19

One boy equals one boy. Two boys equal a half boy. Three boys and the boy disappears said the old wise man. He also said that youth is a great thing but it is a shame it is wasted on those who don't appreciate it.

7.20

Humans are a saintly lot. Humans are an evil lot. We are saints with an incredible capacity to do harm. We are a harmful lot with an incredible capacity to do good.

7.21

Don't pay much attention to those who curse or say less than good things about you. Even more, run the other way when they say something good.

7.22

Be honest with yourself. Every neighborhood has a fool. Be sure to give your neighbor a chance to be one as well.

7.23

Just when I think I understand what life is really all about, the rules change or a new ball is thrown into the mix.

7.24

Who can figure it all out?

7.25

Not me, but I did learn from a proverb that the conflict between right and wrong is the sickness of the mind.

7.26

My friend says that if I have not had an argument today, then I have not spoken to someone today.   I wanted to argue with him that he was wrong.

7.27

Do all the parts add up to get the sum or is the sum just a bunch of parts? Figure this out: How many pancakes will go through a screen door to cover the tin roof of a dog house? Sixteen! Sixteen? How is that?

7.28

Because a bullfrog wrapped in aluminum foil can't drive a milk truck around a cabbage patch.

7.29

See, the Mystery is rather simple to understand but we are always scheming with many schemes about bullfrogs.
Thus spoke Zebediah.

8.1

Common sense has taught me much wisdom. Wisdom has kept me out of a many ditch. But yet, I learned a lot from being in a ditch! So I smile when I am not in a ditch and I try to smile when I am in the ditch.

8.2

Be a person of your word. "Your word is your bond. Use them wisely, not cheaply," the old-timers say. I guess words are cheaper nowadays.

8.3

Uncle Sam will do pretty much what he wants. Just ask Lem and others; they helped to set the record straight.

8.4

Many have gone to Washington D.C. promising to be different declaring, "What are you doing on this Hill? I come to be different." They do come back different; they bring the ways of the Hill back to where they come from.

8.5

When the emperor has no clothes, when is the best time to expose him? The wise will know, maybe.

8.6

Life is heavy and we have cursed the ground and the Creator. Who can blame us?

8.7

Indeed, we do not know what is to be, for who can tell us how it will be?

8.8

If I could control and direct the path of a windstorm, then I could sway or affront the power of death. If I could do both, then am I a god? No one, however, is discharged from the sway of the wind or death. The bad can't stay nor the good, death. As one wise fellow long ago declared, "Death is the Lord."

8.9

A day is long with learning. I learned that the day is long! Some use the longest of the day to hurt, others to create. I reckon that the night does the same but who sees it?

8.10

I went to the funeral of a scoundrel. He was mean, cruel, spiteful and dishonest. When I left the funeral, I left searching for the right funeral because I didn't recognize the man they eulogized.   He had the same name and family of the scoundrel but….

8.11

I have heard it said that you reap what you sow, but the harvest feels as though it is a day of the harvest is October 32nd or it never comes.

8.12

Do those who do evil fear God? Do those who fear God do evil? Do those who fear not the Creator, love less or love more?

8.13

Life is a shadow. Its existence is dependent on a mixture of light and darkness. Should I embrace the light and ignore the darkness? Should I embrace the darkness and ignore the darkness? I will embrace both!

8.14

I read in another book, "There is a vanity that takes place on earth, that there are righteous people who are treated according to the conduct of the wicked, and there are wicked people who are treated according to the conduct of the righteous. I said that this also is vanity." Can't say I disagree.

8.15

Enjoy life! Embrace life! Eat a good and savory meal with a nice cold drink. Enjoy the company of family and friends. Live in the moment, for the past and the future are just that.

8.16

My thoughts keep me awake at night. Some thoughts keep me awake with excitement, others, uncertainty. I want to make sense of everything. I want to know everything. I want to understand everything.

8.17

And then the great Mystery emerged out of the shadows of life. The deeper I dig into the Mystery, I unearth more Mystery. The mist of Crooked Creek comes to mind.
Thus Zebediah spoke.

9.1

I have been thinking about a lot of things. The mist at Crooked Crook never inquires with the content of my heart or the intentions of my mind before it enfolds me. It, like death, culls no one. You would reckon that good follows good and bad follows bad. Everything feels more like a roll of the dice. And is God rolling the dice?

9.2

Death comes to all of us. That mist of death is no respecter of persons. Good, bad, indifferent, passionate, kind, cruel, it does not matter.

9.3

Death swallows all indifferently like a dog long held sustenance.

9.4

Hope pierces the world on the birthing bed. Is there no hope on the death bed?

9.5

Only fools fear death. For death is a threshold which many a soul has crossed. I am not alone in facing the slim line between the living and the dead. Do we forget the dead because they no longer remember themselves?

9.6

If you can only swim in the same river once, is life such a river? The current for both is swift and sure, so,

9.7

Go, enjoy life, embrace your kin, visit unknown places, eat a moon pie and drink a RC cola under a tall oak tree in midsummer. God created us for such things!

9.8

Momma said that I should make sure that I am wearing clean underwear and wash my hair everyday. In all, she was not just teaching me about hygiene.   She was teaching me that I should not just let life happen - I should "will" it.

9.9

Love someone with all the love of your heart, hold nothing back. Given that life is such a mixed bag, you need someone to lean on and someone to share pie.

9.10

Live fiercely.   No need to "white knuckle" life. You cannot embrace anyone or anything with clenched fists.   As the days of life draw nigh, think about what has been embraced because dead hands cannot hold anything living.

9.11

Even a blind hog can find an acorn, so they say. Same goes for us bipeds. Some win. Some lose. Some tie. Life is a roll of the dice but we will the roll!

9.12

Chicken Little has many voices and talking heads. Listen to the voice of your heart for though calamity has many a snare, at least when caught, you will recognize yourself.

9.13

The most wisdom that I have ever witnessed came from a corner of the world where I did not expect. Wisdom is no stranger among us, we just don't recognize it when it bumps into us.

9.14

There are many a story about many a people who, though surrounded by powerful forces, saved their family or community.

9.15

Through their wisdom, great things happened. If you don't believe me, just ask the "Z" man.

9.16

Yet despite those stories, we often defer our wisdom to the fools who amuse ourselves to death. You know who they are. We all know them by their names. But for those who saved a whole community, we long forget.

9.17

Listen to the silent words of the wise more than the loud shouts of the fools.

9.18

Yet, one bad apple can ruin a whole bushel.
Thus spoke Zebediah.

10.1

You can add ice cream to manure but it will not improve the taste of the manure.   Being a quarter of inch off plumb can make a foot of difference. The same goes for foolishness.

10.2

Every journey begins with a single step, in the right direction.

10.3

Even from a long distance, a foolish flea can be seen on the hindquarters of the right leg of a tick hound.

10.4.

Keeping cool under hot conditions will go a long way.

10.5

It does not make much sense and it has hurt a many of folk but,

10.6

Stupidity, if popular, will usually take the high seat but the wise take the back seat.

10.7

I have seen the clowns of politics lead the parade completely naked while everyone snickers but never say word. The wise do, but no one listens.

10.8

When a well is dug, the foolish falls in to test the depth. The child of the fool will be bitten by the caged but dead snake.

10.9

Stones can hurt both your bones and feelings. When working among falling timber, it is better to run first than ask "What?"

10.10

A sharp wit can get you further down the road. A dull one reduces your chances of finding the road.

10.11

One is not much of a snake handler if the snake handles you first.

10.12

Words are quite powerful, just like a rattler; handle with care. It doesn't take long to know the difference between a wise and a foolish handler of words.

10.13

For one, the wise use as few as words as possible, but not the fool.

10.14

"Why use ten words when a thousand will do!" exclaims the foolish. The words of the fool are light as any morning fog hugging the French Broad River. At least the fog knows when to call it quits.

10.15

The lightness of being guides the foolish. Do not take directions from the fool; it will lead down the path that is unbearable.

10.16

God gave the land to nourish both the body and soul of its inhabitants. Eat of the bounty, soak in its beauty. Happy is the land that is led by ones of few words.

10.17

Happy is the land of the people who chose the heaviest weight of being.

10.18

Pa Kettle never fixed the leaking roof when it was not raining because it wasn't leaking. When it did rain, it can't be patched with all that water running down. Pa Kettle later ran for Congress and was elected on many occasions.

10.19.

Festivals are the joys of the heart.   Wine makes one appreciate the heaviest of life and money can't buy love and homegrown tomatoes but it sure will get Sears and Roebuck off your back.

10.20

Be careful with your words, they are not only powerful but they can fly.
One never knows where they land.
Thus Zebediah spoke.

11.1

Random acts of kindness are a good thing. Intentional acts of kindness, however, are even better.   I have been to the Atlantic Ocean at Hunting Island. I once threw a nickel into tide. Years later, while walking on the same shoreline, I found a dime. It is funny how some things come back to you – sometimes double!

11.2.

My maternal grandfather did many things to earn a living. That way, if it rained and he could not bale hay, at least he could haul rock.

11.3

Someone much wiser said that any story can go one way or another, and it usually does.

11.4

It's foolish to broadcast seed in a windstorm, just as it is to hang laundry in the rain. It is good to know the difference.

11.5

We have learned a lot from science and I am delighted to know and learn. However, there is a miracle to life that defies both logic and reason.   There is something behind the facts and it is a Mystery to me!

11.6

Sow your acts in intentional kindness both in the morning and the evening. It will not hurt to do so in between. Whatever you do, on the other hand, do not get attached to the results.

11.7

The warmth of the sun in midwinter seems a distant memory. Embrace the memory and soak in the summer sun so that you can have a memory to embrace in the cold winter.

11.8

The days of life are good and bad.   Sometimes they are real good and other times, real bad. The aesthetic and the moralist all have their say about this but Soren invited me to go a little further.

11.9

"Youth is a great thing but it is a damn shame that it is wasted on those who don't appreciate it," Mr. Ramsey once told me when I was sixteen. I thought that he didn't know what he was talking about.   One of us has learned a lot since that conversation.   Respect the Mystery of life. Hopefully, it will respect us as well. Rejoice, young man, while you are young, and let your heart cheer you in the days of your youth.

11.10

The days drag on but the years fly by.   I learned about the first part of that when I was a teenager awaiting my turn to be an adult. I only learned the latter half in my middle age. I am a slow learner.

Thus spoke Zebediah.

12.1

Respecting the Mystery is easy to do when life is easily accessible but not so when old age sneaks up on me.   Then things are a little more challenging.

12.2

When my eyes grow dim and even glasses no longer let me enjoy seeing the sun set over Mount LeConte, I will try to remember not to forget.

12.3

When I can no longer hold my iced tea because of trembling hands, and when my back is bent over due to weight of the many years of hard work, and when I can no longer enjoy my fried chicken because my teeth are few in number, I soon discover another side of the Mystery.

12.4

With dimmed lights I try to navigate my way around, I now need some to lead me. And why has everyone stopped talking to me, their mouths move but no sound comes out.

12.5

This is strange new land that I wander, quite different from the days of my youth. This land frightens me.   Too many rocks in the road, I don't see them until I stumbled over them. I don't get up as quickly as I used to do.   My hair has changed to the color of my father's. I now need a third leg to help along this road of diminishing desires.   Though this road is unfamiliar to me, multitudes have traveled it.   As I travel it, just like my ancestors, now I see along the road the mourners who come to wish me fairly well.   They now sit on the stump where I once sat as my grandfathers and grandmothers made this trip. I wept for them. Now, there are those who weep for me, or do they?

12.6

Did I weep for my grandparents because I was sad for losing them or did I weep because, deep down, I knew that the same fate awaited me?

12.7

We all return to the loving earth of the mountains and my breath returns to the Mystery from which it came and to which gave it.

12.8

Vanity of vanities, all is vanity, said the Teacher. But I, Zebediah, say that life and death is my own doing. I will both!

12.9

I declare so because Soren "knighted" me when he suggested that I peer deep into the Mystery of life.

12.10

I have tried to speak plainly and not get above my raising.

12.11

The sayings of the Mountain Preacher are sure and tried not because I say so, but because I am sure that I have tried them.

12.12

You can never stop learning. There is some much in our world but the real question is rather simple.

12.13

The end of this matter is rather simple; when will you start living? When you do, it is the act of your will and in turn, an intentional act of respecting the Mystery. For the Mystery is not dead! We have just been dead to the Mystery!

12.14

In my old age, I walk towards that Mystery. Don't weep for me. Weep for those who never start living!

Finally, Zebediah stopped speaking.

The Oak Tree of Enlightenment

It was a hot summer late August afternoon.

I had spent the day with my grandfather. After a morning in the hayfield and riding on the left fender well of his Ford tractor and then a run to the quarry for a load of rock to be delivered to the local manufacturer of burial vaults, we stop at Kitts' Grocery.

We leave the store with two thick cut bologna sandwiches and a cold drink. We did not open the bag of our recent purchases until the dump truck backed into its stall under the shed and we rest beneath the oak tree in my grandfather's yard.

With our backs resting against the trunk of the tree and our bottoms on the ground of fescue grass, my grandfather reaches into the first of the two white grocer bags or "pokes" as he preferred. He hands me my bologna sandwich and balances his sandwich on his right knee. Retrieving the other grocer bag, he pulls out my RC Cola which glistens on the outside with the condensate from the summer heat. Then he lustily pulls out his tall can of Colt 45. After exchange of "drink up," his version of table grace, we simultaneously guzzle our cold drinks. I feel like a real man that afternoon under that tree. It was a macho kind of thing, however. I sit with a man that is far from the sophistication of the local state university, he is locally known at best, and is a man with a seemly lack of organized religiosity but yet full of life. He does things his way. He is far from sainthood, just ask my mother, his second oldest daughter, and the fourth oldest child.

That afternoon, however, has forever been etched if not forged into my memory as though it was yesterday. I look upon it as the day I began to pursue the questions of what is life and its claim on me. I don't know how and I don't know why.

It is said the Buddha had his bodhi tree and Jesus had his wilderness. We all have our starting points of jumping into the Mystery of life. That oak tree in east Knox County Tennessee was my launching point for a life struggle in trying to discern and take full responsibility for my life. As Nietzsche suggested,

> "What, if some day or night a demon were to steal after you into your loneliest loneliness and say to you: 'This life as you now live it and have lived it, you will have to live once more and innumerable times more; and there will be nothing new in it, but every pain and every joy and every thought and sigh and everything unutterably small or great in your life will have to return to you, all in the same succession and sequence—even this spider and this moonlight between the trees, and even this moment and I myself. The eternal hourglass of existence is turned upside down again and again, and you with it, speck of dust!'

Would you not throw yourself down and gnash your teeth and curse the demon who spoke thus? Or have you once experienced a tremendous moment when you would have answered him: 'You are a god and never have I heard anything more divine.' If this thought gained possession of you, it would change you as you are or perhaps crush you. The question in each and every thing, 'Do you desire this once more and innumerable times more?' would lie upon your actions as the greatest weight. Or how well disposed would you have to become to yourself and to life to crave nothing more fervently than this ultimate eternal confirmation and seal?"

Nietzsche makes plenty of declarations through all his writings. However, this weightier matter is more than just a pondering. It is worth exploring.

Is the book of Ecclesiastes making a similar claim on life? Is the book a blunt assertion that every act of life, every detail of it - every viewed sunset and moonlight are just a repeat of a repeat of a repeat? Is the epilogue of Ecclesiastes (12:13-14) a bold yet orthodox theological declaration responding to Nietzsche's demon? Or is Qoheleth actually embracing the God of such recurrence? Furthermore, is the Wesleyan notion of Christian Perfection an embrace of Nietzsche's recurrence or maybe more aptly, is Nietzsche restating Wesley's notion of full sanctification - embracing life fully, perfectly?

Yet, perfect love was never a thought experiment for John Wesley. It is an "attainable" lifestyle that casts out all fears, giving thanks for everything! Perfect love is a bold proclamation - not for the mild of heart or mind as John Wesley discovered despite his conviction that such a notion came from God. Others insisted that the doctrine has less than divine origins.

The mountains of southern Appalachia are just as bold, challenging the everydayness of life. Proclaiming the gospel from the mountain tops takes a special courage and a special language, muses the mountain preacher.

The grandson muses as well.

90379288R00031

Made in the USA
Columbia, SC
03 March 2018

The year was 2001 and Zebediah (God's gift) had been living
on Rich Mountain in the Smoky
Mountains near Townsend, Tennessee. After ten years of solitary study
and meditation in a tucked
away mountain cave, Zebe-
diah felt called by the great
Mystery to come down from
the mountain to share what
was on this mind and heart.
He realized from the outset
that folks would be fixed
on their own ways and their
own ways of thinking and
doing things. He wasn't
descending from the mountain to
gather up a following, however.

Thus begins Thus Spoke Zebediah: Musings of a Mountian
Preacher, A Smoky Mountain Version of the Book of Ecclesiastes.
Confronted with death, living has
it challenges, suggests Zebediah, the
preacher from the Crooked Creek
Congregation of the Tired but True
Believers Church.

Life and death are worth the
pondering. Zebediah speaks...

ISBN 9781460915721

9 781460 915721

90000